About the Book

Story Elements is designed to introduce young readers and writers to the tools that authors use as they create stories. The activities explore the concepts of character, setting, problem (conflict), and plot. The activities focus on the different concepts and progress from easiest to more challenging. In addition, some exercises include fictional stories while others feature nonfiction text.

Pages from this book can be used individually to strengthen the recognition of a specific element, or to introduce it as a topic. Workbook activities can also act as springboards prior to creative writing sessions. Teachers might want to use certain pages on more difficult concepts—such as identifying a story's climax—to help review the material after it has been worked on in class.

• •

Table of Contents

Moving Day

Each Brewster kid feels differently about moving to a new home. Circle a name to answer the first four questions. Then, write the name of the person who you think said each quote.

BILLY   BRENDA   BETTY   BRAD

1.	Who looks angry?	Brad	Betty	Brenda	Billy
2.	Who looks sad?	Brad	Betty	Brenda	Billy
3.	Who looks happy?	Brad	Betty	Brenda	Billy
4.	Who looks worried?	Brad	Betty	Brenda	Billy

5. "When we move to the new house, I will have my own room! I can't wait!" _____

6. "I'm angry! I don't want to leave my home! I have lived here my whole life!" _____

7. "I've heard that my new teacher is very hard. I like our new house but I'm not sure about the school." _____

8. "I'm going to miss playing with all of my friends in the park. Thinking about saying goodbye to them makes me sad." _____

Spotlight on Reading

Story Elements
Grades 3–4

Carson-Dellosa Publishing LLC
Greensboro, North Carolina

Credits

Layout and Cover Design: Van Harris
Development House: The Research Masters

Cover Photo: Image Copyright Dmitriy Shironosov, 2011 Used under license from Shutterstock.com

Visit carsondellosa.com for correlations to Common Core, state, national, and Canadian provincial standards.

Carson-Dellosa Publishing LLC
PO Box 35665
Greensboro, NC 27425 USA
carsondellosa.com

ISBN 978-1-60996-493-1
13-080227784

Brad's Robot

Read the story. Number the events below in the order that they happened in the story.

No one had seen Brad for hours. He was in the basement building a robot. Brad thought his family would be really surprised when they saw it. He hoped they would not be mad because he used many of their things to create it. First, Brad used the trash can from the kitchen for the robot's body. He used his mother's flower pot for the head. A shoe box for his brother's sneakers made the perfect hat.

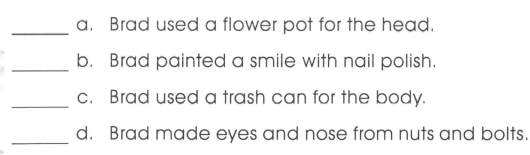

Next, Brad added a fly swatter to make one arm and a broom to make the other. He found some large nuts and bolts in his father's toolbox. He used them to make the robot's eyes and nose. Finally, he painted a smile on the robot with his big sister's nail polish.

When he was finished, Brad took a long look at the robot he had built. He thought it was terrific! He hoped his family would agree.

_____ a. Brad used a flower pot for the head.

_____ b. Brad painted a smile with nail polish.

_____ c. Brad used a trash can for the body.

_____ d. Brad made eyes and nose from nuts and bolts.

_____ e. Brad made one arm from a fly swatter.

_____ f. Brad used a shoe box for a hat.

5

Name _____

Read the story. Answer the questions on page 7.

• •

"OK," said Sara. "Let's take this experiment one step at a time. First, we have to build a volcano with this empty yogurt cup inside of it."

"Let's make it really tall!" said Ahmad. "I will get the bag of sand."

Timothy wrinkled his forehead. "Are you sure we are doing this right?" he asked. "We really do not want to mess this up."

Valerie yawned. "Who cares? It's a silly experiment." She doodled in her notebook while the other three students built the sand volcano.

"Good," said Sara. "Now we mix the red food coloring into this vinegar. The volcano will not be red, but the 'lava' will."

"That's great! This is going to be the coolest thing!" said Ahmad. He bent over to watch Sara mixing the liquids together.

"Ahmad, would you please hold this funnel?" asked Sara. "Valerie, will you put the baking soda in the volcano?"

"*Ummm,* no," said Valerie, rolling her eyes. "I think I will just stand here and watch the rest of you scientists."

"Here, Timothy, you can do it," said Sara. "Just fill it halfway."

"Halfway? Shouldn't we measure it or something?" Tim spooned the powder into the volcano. He frowned. "Nothing is happening. I must have messed it up."

Sara read the instruction sheet. "No, there is no reaction until we pour the vinegar on it," she said.

"I saw a real volcano once in Hawaii," said Ahmad. "The plastic cup is like the underground chamber of the volcano. The red lava is really melted rock that is forced to the surface by hot gases. The lava is red-hot. You can really see it glow at night."

Sara said, "Is everyone ready? I am going to pour in the vinegar now."

Valerie yawned and looked out the window.

Timothy stepped back and chewed his lower lip. "I hope it works."

Ahmad leaned forward to watch. He grinned as the soda 'erupted' over the top of the volcano. "It works!"

Timothy looked unsure. "It is not glowing. Is the lava supposed to glow? Maybe we made a mistake."

"We followed the instructions. I do not think it is supposed to glow," said Sara.

"Let's do it again!" said Ahmad.

Name _____

Write the answers to the questions about "Volcano Adventure."

• •

1. Which character seems most excited about the experiment? _____

2. Which character seems least interested in the experiment? _____

3. Which character seems worried about the experiment? _____

4. Which character seems to take charge of the experiment? _____

5. Each student went home and told his/her parents about the science lab. Write the name of each character next to his/her description.

    a. "We did an experiment where a volcano actually erupted right in class! I was worried it wouldn't work, but it did!" _____

    b. "We did an experiment where we colored vinegar with food coloring and built a volcano model. It was very important that we followed the instructions to make it work." _____

    c. "We built a model of a volcano that worked like the real thing! We actually made a mixture that was red like lava. Then we made the volcano erupt! It was so great, I wanted to do it again!" _____

    d. "We did some kind of science thing. I don't really remember." _____

    _____

6. If you had to pick one of these characters as a lab partner, who would you pick? Write a paragraph explaining why you think that character would make a good lab partner. _____

    _____

    _____

    _____

    _____

The Goldilocks Report

In every story, some characters are more important than others. They are called main characters. Other characters with smaller parts are called minor characters. Read the report and circle the answer to each question.

• •

At 5:05 P.M., we were called to the home of a Mr. and Mrs. Bear. They had been out for the day. Upon returning home, they found the lock on their door had been broken. Officer Paws and I went into the house. We found that food had been eaten and a chair had been broken. Paws searched the backyard while I went upstairs. I found a person asleep in a small bed. The subject was a female human with curly blonde hair. She was unknown to the Bear family. The human claimed her name was Goldilocks. She carried no identification to prove her claim. The subject confessed to trespassing and eating food. She stated that she was sorry for her actions and promised to pay for any food that she ate.

1. In the fairy-tale version of this story, who is the main character?

    Goldilocks   Baby Bear   Papa Bear

2. What characters were added to the story "The Goldilocks Report"?

    Mr. Bear and Baby Bear   Officer Grizzly and Officer Paws

3. Who tells the story "The Goldilocks Report"?

    Goldilocks   Officer Grizzly   Officer Paws

4. In the fairy tale of Goldilocks, which bear has the biggest part?

    Papa Bear   Mama Bear   Baby Bear

5. In the fairy tale of Goldilocks, which one is a minor character?

    Papa Bear   Goldilocks   Officer Paws

6. In "The Goldilocks Report," which one is a minor character?

    Officer Paws   Officer Grizzly   Goldilocks

Name _____

Read the story. Use all of the words from the Word Bank to describe the plot of the story.

● ●

Word Bank				
spider	jar	apartment	rain	afternoon

Shawn walked slowly up the steps to his apartment. It had been raining for three days and did not seem likely to stop. There were puddles in the street and all over the sidewalk.

Shawn's mother had picked him up at school. She was parking the car as he walked into their apartment. Shawn wiped his shoes on the mat outside the door. Suddenly, he saw a spider. The spider was black and hairy with a fat, round body and eight long legs. She was big too, and was almost the size of his palm.

The spider was walking up the side of the wall. But when she saw Shawn, she stopped in her tracks. They stared at one another.

Shawn's mother came up the stairs. As she reached the apartment door, she took a big step back. "What's wrong?" Shawn asked.

Shawn's mother pointed to the spider. "What is that?" she cried.

"Oh!" Shawn replied. "That's just a trapdoor spider, Mom. We studied them in class and they're harmless. All of this rain must have flooded her home."

Shawn's mother sighed in relief. She unlocked the front door and helped Shawn find a clean jar under the kitchen sink. They were going to make a temporary home for the spider until the rain stopped. They would need to add some grass and soil to make it cozy for the spider.

"I think we should keep her until the rain stops," Shawn said. As the spider crawled into the jar, he thought that it was not a boring afternoon after all.

_____

_____

_____

_____

_____

_____

The Journey West

Read the journal entries of Abigail. She was a pioneer girl who traveled west with her family to a new home in Nebraska. Answer the questions on page 11.

● ●

May 12, 1871
Today, we left our dear home in Ohio forever. Oh, how Grandmother cried as we said goodbye! Uncle Dan and Aunt Martha have bought our farm. It is no longer our home. When we drove past the woods at the west edge of our fields, Papa said, "Take a good look at those trees. It will be many years before we have that many trees near us again." I tried to be brave. But later, I went in the back of the wagon and cried softly to myself.

June 10, 1871
When we got to the Mississippi River, Mama paid for our crossing. Papa went to meet the other people with whom we will travel in our wagon train. The Mississippi is wide, fast, and dangerous. I stood on the shore and wondered what might happen if the ferry was not strong. It was a good raft, but Mama's face was pale. The horses did not like it one bit.

June 14, 1871
It seems awful to be traveling among strangers. I have never been in a place where I did not know everyone. Now every night when we camp, there are new people eating dinner with us. It makes me feel very shy. The adults talk about land prices. They say that they will be able to buy twice the land they had in the East. Meanwhile, I just steal glances at the other children. I have not talked to one of them.

July 12, 1871
Every day, I walk beside the wagon. It is easier than being jolted around inside. Today, Mandy Peterson was walking and saw a rattlesnake! It came so close that it almost bit her. Luckily, she jumped away in time. Mama told me to get in the wagon, and I did at once. Mandy should not have been walking in this tall grass without boots. I will make sure that I always wear mine.

August 5, 1871
We reached Lincoln, Nebraska today, and I began to feel better. It is a much nicer town than I had expected. Several families have already moved there and built their own cabins. There is also a general store that sells supplies, seeds, cloth, and even a corncob doll. I think it will not be so bad to call this place "home."

Name _____

The Journey West (cont.)

Answer the questions about Abigail and her feelings about her trip.

• •

1. How does Abigail feel about leaving her home in Ohio?

    _____

2. Does Abigail like to meet new people? _____
    What proof do you have from the story for your answer?

    _____

3. How does Abigail feel when she arrives at Lincoln, Nebraska?

    _____

4. Circle four adjectives that seem to describe Abigail the best:

    friendly   adventurous   shy

    scared   obedient   strong-willed

    curious   bold   homesick

5. What words does Abigail use to describe the Mississippi River?

    _____   _____   _____

6. Why do you think Abigail's father is leaving Ohio to farm in Nebraska?

    _____

7. Do you think Abigail will have an easy time or a hard time in her new
    home?_____
    Give a reason for your answer.

    _____

    _____

8. Would you like to have gone west on a wagon train?_____
    Give a reason for your answer.

    _____

    _____

© Carson-Dellosa

Name _____

Read the story. Answer questions about it below.

• •

The smallest bear at the North Pole was also the loneliest bear at the North Pole. He was too small to play with the older bears. His parents worried that he might get hurt if he did. So, he spent each day wishing for a friend his own size.

Then one day, he watched the older bears building snowmen. Suddenly, the little bear knew how to solve his problem. So, he spent an entire day building a snow bear that looked just like him. It was the same size that he was. So, he was not the only little bear at the North Pole.

The smallest bear wrapped a scarf around his snow friend's neck. He also placed a warm hat on its head. The smallest bear realized that he could not take his snow friend inside his house. So, he ran inside, grabbed an old blanket, and collected his toys. He spread the blanket out on the snow and laid his toys on top.

The smallest bear spent the whole winter playing and laughing with the snow bear. He never felt lonely, not even for a minute. But then, the spring air came to the North Pole. It melted all of the snow and the snow bear dissolved into a puddle.

At first, the smallest bear was sad. He missed his friend! But, as he knelt down to the puddle, he saw his own reflection. He realized that he had grown over the winter months. He was no longer the smallest bear. Even better, he would no longer be the loneliest bear! Now, he was big enough to play with the others. He ran off to join them.

1. When does the story take place? _____

2. Where does the story take place? _____

3. Describe the setting of this story. _____

   _____

4. How does the character change his surroundings? _____

   _____

   _____

Name _____

Times and Travels

The setting of a story may include both a place and a time. The time of a setting may be a period of history, a special day, or a season. Use the Word Bank to choose the setting for each paragraph below.

• •

Word Bank

autumn	ancient Rome
Egyptian desert	winter
medieval England	summer

1. Elsie still had a mile to walk to school, and her boots were already wet. The shawl her mother had wrapped over her patched coat was not keeping Elsie warm.

   Setting: _____

2. "There they are, son," Jacob's father said quietly. Jacob's eyes widened. He forgot about the long trip, the blazing sun, and even the camel ride. Nothing mattered except these vast pyramids of stone.

   Setting: _____

3. Ramon and Rosa worked together to build a sand castle. They scooped up buckets of sand. Then they piled the sand together and molded it into a shape. Ramon carved a moat around their castle. Rosa sculpted a tower on each side. They got hot and sweaty in the warm sun. But they did not care because they were having so much fun.

   Setting: _____

4. Sara sighed as she started to rake leaves. They had fallen outside her home. There were piles of orange, yellow, and brown leaves all over the yard. It was her job to gather them into piles and then throw them away. It would take at least an hour to finish. Sara hated this time of year!

   Setting: _____

5. Sir Cedric picked up his helmet calmly as Christopher held the heavy lance. "This joust will be attended by the king," Sir Cedric told his page. "If I do well, I may gain the favor of his majesty."

   Setting: _____

6. Marcus stopped and smoothed down the folds of his toga before entering the temple. He stopped again as he saw Augustus Cyrillus, the new senator, stride up the steps before him.

   Setting: _____

New World, Old World

Sometimes the same setting can create different feelings in different characters. Read the two passages below. Answer the questions on page 15.

Constance Hopkins leaned on the weathered rail of the Mayflower. She gazed across the water. Everything was still. First there was the gray water. Beyond it was a thin band of gold sand, and then the trees. There were no houses, no bridges, no chimneys, no smoke, and no shops. In her mind, she could still see London. That is the great city where she used to live with her father, who was a tanner. Constance thought about the tiny row of huts that they would build when they arrived. What a difference! Her hands gripped the railing as she thought of her life in the years to come. It would be a new life of freedom. "It will be hard at first," she thought. "But we will find the way, just as we found the way to this new world. Here, we will be free to live as we choose."

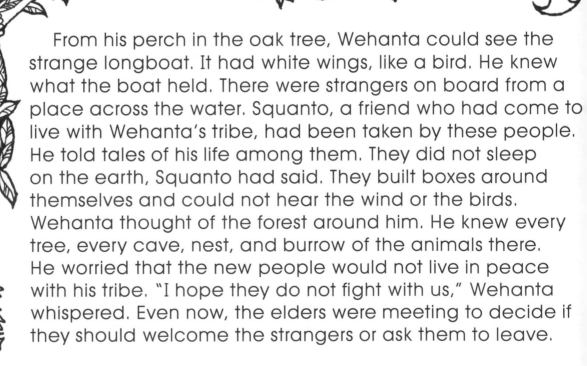

From his perch in the oak tree, Wehanta could see the strange longboat. It had white wings, like a bird. He knew what the boat held. There were strangers on board from a place across the water. Squanto, a friend who had come to live with Wehanta's tribe, had been taken by these people. He told tales of his life among them. They did not sleep on the earth, Squanto had said. They built boxes around themselves and could not hear the wind or the birds. Wehanta thought of the forest around him. He knew every tree, every cave, nest, and burrow of the animals there. He worried that the new people would not live in peace with his tribe. "I hope they do not fight with us," Wehanta whispered. Even now, the elders were meeting to decide if they should welcome the strangers or ask them to leave.

New World, Old World (cont.)

Circle the correct answers to the questions about the story on page 14.

• •

1. What is the setting of the story?

    Leyden   London

    New World   New Amsterdam

2. Why does this setting seem like a new world to Constance?

    There are no trees.   There are no buildings or shops.

    There are no ships.   There are no birds.

3. Why does this setting seem like an old world to Wehanta?

    His people have fought there.   His tribe is large.

    He knows every tree in the forest.   He knows about the ocean.

4. What information does Wehanta have that Constance does not have?

    He has a map of her home, and she does not know where he lives.

    He knows why her people have come to his land, and she does not.

    He has heard stories about her people, and she does not know about his tribe.

5. If Constance's family had traveled to another city in England instead of to the "new world," what would be the biggest change in "New World, Old World"?

    Constance would not be on a ship.

    Constance's father would not be a tanner.

    Wehanta would not be a character in the story.

    Wehanta would not have heard about Constance's people from Squanto.

15

Making a Difference

Read the poem. Circle the answer for each question.

. . . .

If Grandma's home was in the big city
Instead of a forest, so deep, dark, and pretty,
Then Little Red Riding Hood would have no fuss
With the Big Bad Wolf on a city bus.
If Cinderella had run to the mall
Instead of going to the ball,
She might have tried on new blue jeans
Instead of filling a prince's dreams.

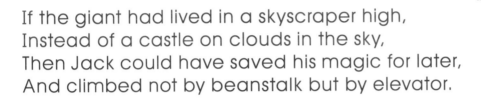

If the giant had lived in a skyscraper high,
Instead of a castle on clouds in the sky,
Then Jack could have saved his magic for later,
And climbed not by beanstalk but by elevator.

1. Which character would seem out of place in a big city?

    a little girl   a grandmother   a wolf

2. If Cinderella had not gone to the ball, how does the poem say she might have spent her time?

    doing chores   looking for a prince   buying clothes

3. In which situation does the setting tell you the story will be make-believe?

    A boy rides an elevator to the top floor.

    A boy climbs a giant beanstalk to a castle in the sky.

    A boy climbs stairs to a second floor apartment.

4. What is a good title for this poem?

    Little Red Riding Hood's Adventure   Settings Can Create Adventures

    Story Settings Do Not Change   Cinderella Goes Shopping

Name _____

The setting of a story affects what the characters wear, how they speak, what they own, and where they live. Underline the sentence in each paragraph where the details do not fit with the setting. Complete the matching activity below the paragraphs.

• •

1. Jason looked at the gray coastline. His journey to find the Golden Fleece had been long and tiring. He bent down to tie one of his sandals. Then he glanced at his wristwatch. Suddenly one of the sailors shouted and pointed!

2. Young Abe Lincoln sat close to the roaring fire. He opened the book he had brought home from school and began to read. He looked up as he heard the weather report on the radio. There was a big snowstorm on its way.

3. The page entered the hall of King Arthur and bowed low. "I have news for you, my lord," he said, holding out a text message. "I believe Sir Galahad may have found the treasure we seek." The king squinted to read the words in the flickering torchlight.

4. Wendy sighed. She had so much work to do on her book report. She flicked on her computer and stared as it booted up. She really wanted to look at a new web site that Kim had told her about, but she knew she needed to do her homework first. She drew the oil lamp closer and started typing.

5. The Great Hall was ready for the winter feast. Fresh straw had been spread on the floor, and the tables were set with bowls, spoons, and drinking cups. The servants hurried to set up strings of tiny electric lights across the mantle. The lord of the manor had even hired pipers to play. The huge log was ready to be hauled to the fireplace, where it would burn for the next 12 days.

6. A square dance in pioneer days ___

7. A classroom today _____

8. A deserted island _____

9. A city on Mars _____

a.   A palm tree

b.   A fan and parasol

c.   A teacher's grade book

d.   A space transporter

Name _____

Read the story. Answer questions about it on the next page.

• •

Maria Ramos had wanted just one thing ever since her first year at Washington Street School. She wanted to win a Costume Day prize. The best costume in each grade wins a prize. Last year, the winners got puzzles and games and books. Maria just had to win this year!

Maria thought and thought about what costume to wear. She looked through magazines and books to get ideas. She looked in shops and at catalogs, too. Maria wanted a special costume that would be different from the rest.

One day, Maria was writing a report on mammals for science class. She saw a picture that gave her a great idea. She would dress as a cow! She bought a tail, horns, and a cowbell from a costume store with her allowance money. Then, she painted black spots onto a white leotard and tights. Finally, she painted hooves onto an old pair of black shoes. After the paint dried, she tried on her costume and looked in the mirror. It was perfect!

At last, the big day came. Costume Day was in the school yard on a Saturday in October. Everyone came to see the costumes. Plus, there were balloons, game booths, and lots of good things to eat. Maria marched in the costume parade with the other students in her grade. She saw kids dressed as superheroes. She also saw kids dressed as clowns. But no one was dressed as a cow like Maria. Most of the costumes were also bought from a store. Only a few were mainly homemade, like Maria's.

After the parade, the principal announced the winners in each class. Would the principal call her name? Maria crossed all of her fingers. She even tried to cross her toes. Then she wished as hard as she could.

"And now for the fourth-grade class," Principal Chin said. "The winner is . . . David Hoffman!" Maria could not believe it. She lost! She had wanted to win so badly. But, she put on a brave face and clapped for her friend David, who was dressed as a doctor.

After all the class winners were announced, Maria started to turn away. Suddenly, the principal said, "We're doing something a little different this year. We're also giving out a grand prize." Maria turned back to hear more. "And the winner of the grand prize will receive a free pass to the fair."

Name _____

Answer questions about the story you just read.

- -

"Oooh," the crowd said. That sounded like an amazing prize. Maria did not dare to think that she would win. One of the older kids would probably get the grand prize. She got ready to put on a brave face and clap again.

"The winner of the Costume Day grand prize is . . . Maria Ramos." She did it! She won! Maria ran up to the stage and excitedly shook Principal Chin's hand. Everyone in the crowd smiled and clapped for her.

Maria did not even think about the free pass to the fair. She was just so happy and proud that she had achieved her goal. She was one of the winners on Costume Day. There was just one question in her head: what costume would she wear next year?

1. What does Maria want? _____

_____

_____

2. What does Maria do to get what she wants? _____

_____

_____

3. What happens to Maria at the end of the story? _____

_____

_____

Number the events in the order they happened in the story.

_____ a. Maria tries on her costume in the mirror.

_____ b. Maria buys a tail, horns, and a cowbell.

_____ c. The principal announces the grand-prize winner.

_____ d. David Hoffman wins the fourth-grade prize.

_____ e. Maria looks in magazines to get ideas.

Ready for the Playoff

Read the story. Answer questions about it on the next page.

• •

Austin was so excited about the baseball playoff that afternoon. For the first time, Coach Greene was going to let Austin be the catcher. In fact, Austin was so excited, he was not paying attention to the model volcano that he and Ping were building in science class.

"Do you want to tear the strips or dip them in paste and put them on?" Ping asked.

"Home run!" Austin replied.

"Huh?" Ping said. He wore a puzzled look on his face.

Austin's faced burned with embarrassment. "I'm sorry. I was thinking about the game."

Ping laughed. "Oh!" he said. "Well, that explains it. Do you think we'll win?"

"My big brother says our school hasn't won a playoff in at least five years. Maybe we finally will," Austin replied.

Austin saw Mrs. Jackson walking toward them. Austin picked up a piece of newspaper and tore it into strips. "I guess we better get back to work."

Ping agreed. He dipped a strip into paste and smoothed it onto the side of the model volcano.

As the boys kept adding strips to the volcano, they began to enjoy the work. It was interesting to see the volcano take shape. Before they knew it, Mrs. Jackson was announcing to the class, "Time to start cleaning up. After all, you don't want to be late for the game."

Austin and Ping looked at one another. They excitedly gave each other a high-five. Then they quickly put the lid on the container of paste and bagged up the extra newspaper. They carried their model to the science table and wiped down their work area. They were back in their seats and ready to go in two minutes.

Austin watched the clock. It would not be long now. A few minutes later, the bell rang. Everyone in class cheered. Austin yelled the loudest of all. It was time for the game, and he was ready for the playoff!

Story Elements • CD-104557

Name _____

Answer questions about the story you just read. Circle the correct letter.

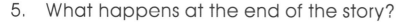

1. Who is the main character in the story?
   a. Austin
   b. Mrs. Lee
   c. Coach Greene

2. What does the main character want?
   a. to make a model volcano
   b. to be a catcher in the playoff
   c. to clean up the science classroom

3. Where does the story take place?
   a. on another planet
   b. on a baseball field
   c. in a classroom

4. When does the story take place?
   a. now
   b. a long time ago
   c. in the future

5. What happens at the end of the story?
   a. Austin's team wins the playoff.
   b. The boys start working on a model volcano.
   c. Science class ends as the bell rings.

The Story of Clara Pickle

Read the story. Complete an activity about it on the next page.

• •

Everyone knew Clara Pickle. She lived on a farm on the edge of town. Clara Pickle was as dear and sweet as anyone could be. In fact, it was her good nature that often got her into trouble.

One day, a gray cat wandered into Clara's kitchen. Clara, who lived alone, decided to keep the cat as a pet. She was glad for the company. The next morning, she let the cat out for a breath of fresh air. When the cat came back that afternoon, he was no longer alone. He had brought his entire family and most of his friends with him. There were 34 cats in all!

Clara, sweet person that she was, adopted them all. In the next few days, the 34 cats had each added a few friends. Clara Pickle then had 92 cats and kittens! She decided that 92 cats was a few too many. So, she moved many of them to the barn near her house. She gave a few dozen cats to some of her friends too. They were also glad to have the company.

But Clara kept the first gray cat. He was her favorite. Clara named him Dilly and gave him a nice bed on the floor next to her own. She loved to listen to him purr at night as she was falling asleep.

Name _____

Number the events below to retell the story in the correct sequence.

• •

_____ a. Clara had 92 cats and kittens.

_____ b. Clara gave the gray cat a bed next to hers.

_____ c. Clara took in a gray cat.

_____ d. A gray cat wandered into Clara's kitchen.

_____ e. The gray cat returned with his family and friends.

_____ f. Clara gave some of the cats to her friends.

_____ g. Clara let out the gray cat for some fresh air.

_____ h. Clara moved some of the cats to her barn.

Woodie Lost and Found

Read the story. Answer questions about it on page 25.

• •

Woodie was scared. For the second time in her young life, she was lost. When the branch fell on her little house and fence, she had just barely escaped. She scrambled across her pen as quick as lightning. The thunder crashed, and Woodie leaped across the fallen fence into the woods. Now the rain poured down. The wind howled. The little woodchuck shivered under a big oak tree. She did not know what to do.

When Woodie was a baby, she had gotten lost in the woods. She could not find food for herself. She hurt her paw, and she spent hours licking it to make it feel better. All day, she scratched at a small hole in the ground to try to make a burrow. This made her even more hungry.

But then one day, Rita had found her. Rita had knelt down by Woodie's badly made burrow and held out an apple. Slowly, Woodie limped out and took the apple. It was the best thing she had ever tasted in her life. Rita took the baby woodchuck to the wildlife center where Woodie had lived ever since. Most of the animals at the wildlife center were orphans. Rita taught them how to live in the wild and then let them go when they were ready. But Woodie's paw did not heal well, and Rita knew Woodie would never able to live in the wild like other woodchucks. So Rita made Woodie a small house at the wildlife center. Woodie even had a job; she visited schools with Rita so that students could learn all about woodchucks.

But now the storm had ruined Woodie's house. Scared by the loud crash, Woodie had run so fast that she had gone into the woods by mistake. Woodie did not know how to find her way back home again. Where was Rita?

At dawn, the rain ended. Woodie came to a big stream. She drank some water. She sniffed the air. Maybe the center was across the stream. Woodie jumped onto a rock and then hopped to another one. She landed on her bad paw and fell into the fast-moving water. She struggled to keep her nose above water. The current tossed her against a tangle of broken branches from the storm. Woodie clung to the branches with all her might.

"There she is!" Woodie heard Rita's voice. She saw Rita with Ben, another worker from the center. Rita waded over to the branches. In moments, Woodie was safe in Rita's arms. Rita wrapped a blanket around the tired, soaking-wet woodchuck. Woodie purred her thanks. By the time Ben pulled the van into the parking lot at the wildlife center, Woodie was fast asleep.

Name _____

Circle the answer for each question about the story on page 24.

• •

1. What was the problem in the story "Woodie Lost and Found"?
    a. Woodie hurt her paw.
    b. Woodie had been lost as a baby.
    c. Woodie got lost during a big storm.

2. Who is the main character in the story?

    a. Rita, the wildlife expert
    b. Woodie, a woodchuck
    c. Ben, a wildlife center worker

3. What happens right before Woodie gets lost in the storm?
    a. She is unable to dig a burrow for herself.
    b. Rita loses Woodie on a trip to a school.
    c. The fence of Woodie's pen falls down in the storm.

4. Why do you think we are told about Woodie's life as a baby?
    a. so we know that Woodie has been lost before—she knows what to do
    b. so we know that Woodie cannot live in the wild—she is in danger
    c. so we know Woodie trusts people—she knows if she waits, someone will always come to find her

5. What is the climax of the story?
    a. A branch falls on Woodie's house and she barely gets out in time.
    b. Woodie shivers under a big oak, all alone in the storm.
    c. Woodie falls into the water as she tries to cross a stream.

6. What is the solution/resolution of the story?
    a. Rita finds Woodie under the tree and gives her an apple.
    b. Rita finds Woodie, rescues her from the stream, and takes her home.
    c. Rita finds Woodie and takes her on a visit to a school.

7. What facts do we find out about woodchucks in the story? (Circle all that apply).
    a. Woodchuck babies do not really need their parents.
    b. Woodchucks like apples.
    c. Woodchucks can run very fast.

A Mystery in the Night

Read the story. Answer the questions on page 27.

• •

On a rainy night in October 1857, Joshua finally found the answer to the mystery. So many times, he had asked his mother about doors closing and steps creaking in the night. She had said, "You must have been dreaming, son." So many times, he had asked his father about the sound of horses in the night. He had said, "It must have been closer to morning than you thought, Josh." But on this night, Joshua knew he was not dreaming and was not wrong about the time.

When he heard the kitchen door close, he got out of bed. He walked slowly down the stairs. In the hall, he saw the dim light of a single candle. Then he was face to face with his father. Behind his father stood three people: a man, a woman, and a child. They looked tired and scared, and there were leaves clinging to their clothes. Their skin was dark and their eyes were wide at the sight of Joshua.

"Son, go to your room," said Joshua's father in a stern voice. Joshua backed down the hall, still looking. Later, Joshua's mother came into his room. "We were wrong to lie to you," she said softly. "You are old enough to know the truth. Your father and I are running a station on the Underground Railroad."

Joshua caught his breath. He had heard about this at school. Some people who felt that slavery was wrong were helping slaves to escape. The slaves made their way from place to place. At each "station" they were given food, water, and help to the next friendly place.

"That family is eating supper now," said his mother. "Tomorrow night, after they rest, your father will drive them to Smith's Landing. Someone will meet them there."

Joshua nodded. His mother looked at him and said, "Do you understand, Joshua? Do you know that you must never say a word about this to anyone?"

Joshua understood. He knew that his father could be put in jail for helping slaves to escape because it was against the law. He would not tell anyone, not even his best friend, James. Joshua and James had talked about the Underground Railroad. They had wondered if anyone they knew was working with the secret organization. Joshua longed to tell James his secret, but he knew he had to keep his promise. His father and mother were doing a good thing and protecting other people. Now, he had to protect his parents and keep his family safe.

A Mystery in the Night (cont.)

Write **first**, **second**, **third**, **fourth**, or **fifth** to show the order of the events in "A Mystery in the Night" from page 26.

• •

When he became adult, Joshua learned more about the help his parents had given. They had been part of the Underground Railroad. That was the name for a secret group of paths and safe houses. Slaves traveled secretly from place to place until they reached freedom. The houses where they stayed were called stations. Guides, like Joshua's parents, were known as conductors. Thousands of slaves traveled the Underground Railroad to freedom in the 1800s.

_____ 1. Joshua decides not to tell James about his parents and their work to help escaped slaves.

_____ 2. Joshua goes down the stairs and into the back hallway.

_____ 3. Joshua sees his father with a family of escaped slaves.

_____ 4. Joshua is told that the noises he hears at night are just his imagination.

_____ 5. Joshua's mother tells him that their house is a station on the Underground Railroad.

"A Mystery in the Night" is only part of a story. Write before or after next to each event to show when it would take place in relation to the part of the story you have read.

_____ 6. Joshua and James hear about a secret organization called "The Underground Railroad" from some of their classmates.

_____ 7. Joshua's father drives the slave family to Smith's Landing.

_____ 8. Joshua wonders if he really dreamed the strange sound of voices coming from the kitchen one night.

_____ 9. James and Joshua go fishing and wonder if anyone they know is helping slaves to escape from the South.

_____ 10. Joshua's mother mends some old clothes but will not tell Joshua why she is fixing the clothing.

27

The Fox and the Grapes

Read the story. Circle the answers to the first three questions. Write answers for the last two questions on the lines.

· ·

On a hot summer's day, a red fox went for a walk. He soon became very thirsty under the scorching sun. He looked for a pond, or a brook, or even a puddle from which to drink, but he had no luck. Then he spied a fat bunch of juicy grapes. They were ripening on a vine which was hanging over a high branch. "Just the thing to quench my thirst," Fox thought.

Fox took a running jump at the grapes, but he missed. He stepped back a few paces. He eyed the grapes greedily, gathered his strength, and leaped for the grapes. His nose brushed the grapes and smelled their sweet scent, but he could not reach them. Fox tried again and again. He jumped and jumped until he could jump no more. Finally, he gathered what energy he had left and tried to climb the tree. He slid down the trunk and landed in a sad heap on the ground.

After a few moment's rest, Fox mustered his dignity and trotted down the path. He declared to himself and any who could hear him, "I am sure those grapes are sour anyway."

1. What was the fox's problem?

    a. He was thirsty.   b. He was hungry.   c. He was lonely.

2. What did the fox find to solve his problem?

    a. a pond   b. a puddle   c. a fat bunch of juicy grapes

3. How did the fox first try to reach the grapes?

    a. by climbing the tree   b. by jumping for them   c. by knocking them out of the tree

4. Was the fox able to solve his problem? What did he do?_____

    _____

5. "The Fox and the Grapes" is a fable by Aesop. The moral of the tale is "It is easy to reject what you cannot have." How does this apply to the fox and his problem?_____

    _____

    _____

    _____

Name _____

Laura Ingalls Wilder

Read the following information about Laura Ingalls Wilder. In the activity below, write **P** after the sentence if it tells about a problem in Laura's family history. Write **S** if the sentence tells about a solution to a problem.

•   •

Laura Ingalls Wilder wrote eight books about her childhood. She grew up in Wisconsin, Kansas, Minnesota, and South Dakota in the 1800s. During her life, she and her family faced many problems.

The Ingalls family lost their farm in Kansas. By mistake, they had built it on land that belonged to an Osage tribe. The family had worked hard to build a house and barn. But they had to leave it and find somewhere else to live.

Several years later, the Ingalls family moved to Minnesota. They lived in a dugout while they built another farm. During this time, Laura's sister Mary became sick. Her eyes were damaged, and she became blind. Laura and her family worked hard to raise money for Mary. When they finally had enough, they sent Mary to a school for blind students. There, she learned how to read braille. She also learned other skills to help her have a better life.

Later, Laura's family moved to South Dakota. They claimed land both in town and out on the prairie. Laura and her sisters liked their new home and neighbors. But life on the prairie could be dangerous.

One winter, the trains could not get through the snow to deliver food. Everyone in town almost starved to death. Laura's future husband, Almanzo, risked his life to help. He traveled to a distant farm to get wheat. The townspeople used the wheat to make bread. It was their only food for the rest of the winter. When spring came, the trains finally arrived and the town was saved.

_____ 1.   The family sent Mary to a school for blind people.

_____ 2.   Trains could not reach Laura's town one snowy winter.

_____ 3.   The Ingalls family settled on land that actually belonged to the Osage tribe.

_____ 4.   Almanzo risked his life to help get wheat from a farm.

_____ 5.   Mary Ingalls went blind after she became ill.

_____ 6.   In the spring, the trains arrived with supplies for the town.

Jorge's Tadpoles

Read the story. Answer questions about it on page 31.

• •

Jorge sat cross-legged on the dusty window seat. He stared at the foggy woods. How he wished he was back in New Mexico! At that moment, he would probably be playing air hockey with his friends, Carlos and Dustin.

Jorge's family had moved to California at the beginning of the year. He had not made even one new friend in two whole months. His sadness felt selfish. Everyone else in his family was so happy in their new home.

Jorge's sister, Anita, had found a kitten in the woods outside their home. His mother had let her keep it. His father has a great new job at the local television station. He loves telling the family about all of the celebrities he meets. His mother likes to go running on the nearby beach every morning. She was also taking classes at the community college in the afternoons. Everyone was having a great time—everyone except for Jorge, that is.

Jorge did not know what to do. None of the boys in his class lived nearby. Besides, they all had known each other since kindergarten. Jorge was an outsider. The boys were polite enough. They could even be friendly. But after they said hello in the morning, they wandered off into groups. He was never included. Jorge could not blame them. He and his old friends had done the same thing lots of times.

Jorge decided to stop feeling so sad. Friends or no friends, it was a perfectly good Saturday afternoon. He opened the back door and stepped outside. The tall trees smelled spicy in the sea air. Jorge began to feel better. He took the back stairs two at a time. He hurried down the familiar path into the woods. A carpet of fallen leaves cushioned his step.

Jorge was surprised when he reached the creek. Something had changed. Water no longer tumbled over the rocks. There were only small pools where the creek should be. He looked carefully into the pools of water. He could see they were filled with tiny, dark creatures. They were packed closely together. They could hardly move through the small amount of water.

Jorge could tell right away that the creatures were tadpoles. He had studied them in science class last year. A few of them had grown back legs. But, they were not yet ready to live on land.

Jorge's Tadpoles (cont.)

Answer questions about the story you just read. Circle the correct letter.

• •

The remaining water was drying up fast. Suddenly, Jorge understood why everyone on the news was talking about a drought. Hardly any rain had fallen in the past month. The water in town was getting very low.

Jorge could not make it rain. But he could help some of the tadpoles. He hurried back to his house to get a glass jar. When he returned, he scooped up some of the tadpoles with the water. As he held up the jar, he could see them swimming around inside.

Jorge decided to take the tadpoles to school on Monday morning. He was sure that his science teacher, Mrs. Abdul, would know how to help them. The other students were excited to see the tadpoles. They gathered around to study them in the jar.

Mrs. Abdul came up with a plan to help the tadpoles. She found a tank to raise them in. She asked Jorge to help her fill it with water. Then, the class put together a schedule to feed the tadpoles and care for them. Everyone would take turns helping out, and Jorge would organize everything.

All of the students enjoyed taking care of Jorge's tadpoles. They learned a lot about frogs and how they grow. They also learned a lot about Jorge and his life back in New Mexico. By the time the last tadpole turned into a frog, Jorge had lots of new friends.

1. Who is the main character in the story?
    a. Jorge
    b. Dustin
    c. Mrs. Abdul

2. What does the main character want?
    a. to learn about tadpoles
    b. to find a kitten
    c. to make friends

3. Where does the story take place?
    a. in California
    b. in New Mexico
    c. in the South

4. When does the story take place?
    a. a long time ago
    b. in the future
    c. now

5. What happens at the end of the story?
    a. Jorge finds tadpoles in the woods.
    b. Jorge's class helps raise the tadpoles.
    c. Jorge learns that tadpoles grow into frogs.

Bitsy's Bad Summer

Read the story. Fill in the web on page 33.

• •

   Bitsy was a gray squirrel who lived in an oak tree behind a yellow house. Her home was a nice, dry nest built of twigs. Bitsy lined the nest with soft fur and feathers. Each day, she gathered nuts and bark for her supper. Bitsy hid tasty acorns so she would have food in the winter. When she could, Bitsy dined upon mushrooms, grasses, and seeds. Sometimes, she scurried up the neighbor's bird feeder for a snack. Bitsy drank from the little stream that meandered through the woods, or she lapped dew on leaves and grass. Bitsy enjoyed her quiet life.

   One summer day, a tall woman moved into the yellow house. She carried a fat, black cat with leaf-green eyes. Bitsy knew a few cats. A multicolored cat lived in the house next door. That cat stayed inside and watched birds from the windowsill. An orange tabby cat sometimes wandered into Bitsy's yard to lounge in the sun-dappled grass. Once, Bitsy ran right up to the orange cat's nose. The cat reached a lazy paw towards Bitsy, but she was too slow to scare Bitsy. The black cat was different.

   Every morning, the tall woman opened the door. The cat she called Midnight, stalked outside and crouched beneath the oak tree. She stared at Bitsy with her leaf-green eyes. Bitsy flicked her tail and scolded the cat. Midnight coiled, ready to spring, her black tail swishing back and forth. Bitsy sensed danger. Late in the evening, the woman opened the door for Midnight. By the time the cat was safely inside, it was time for Bitsy to snuggle up in her nest, safe from predators that hunt in the dark.

   Midnight kept Bitsy from burying acorns and dining on seeds and mushrooms on the ground. Once, Bitsy raced down her tree to bury an acorn before the cat saw her. The tip of a sharp claw raked Bitsy's tail as she raced back up the tree. "Too close!" she thought. "I must be clever, or I will starve!"

   Early the next morning, Bitsy scurried down the tree to search for food before Midnight returned. When the door opened, and Midnight took up her post beneath the oak, Bitsy jumped from branch to branch, climbing along fences and rooftops in search of safe places to eat and drink. She was constantly alert to dangers from wild animals and pets. She sniffed the air for dogs and cats. She kept her ears and eyes open for foxes, raccoons, and hawks. It was hard work, but she did not starve.

   One day, when the leaves were changing colors, the tall woman packed her bags and her cat in the car and drove away. Bitsy raced up and down her tree in celebration. Her bad summer was over at last!

Bitsy's Bad Summer (cont.)

Fill in the web below with information from the story on page 32.

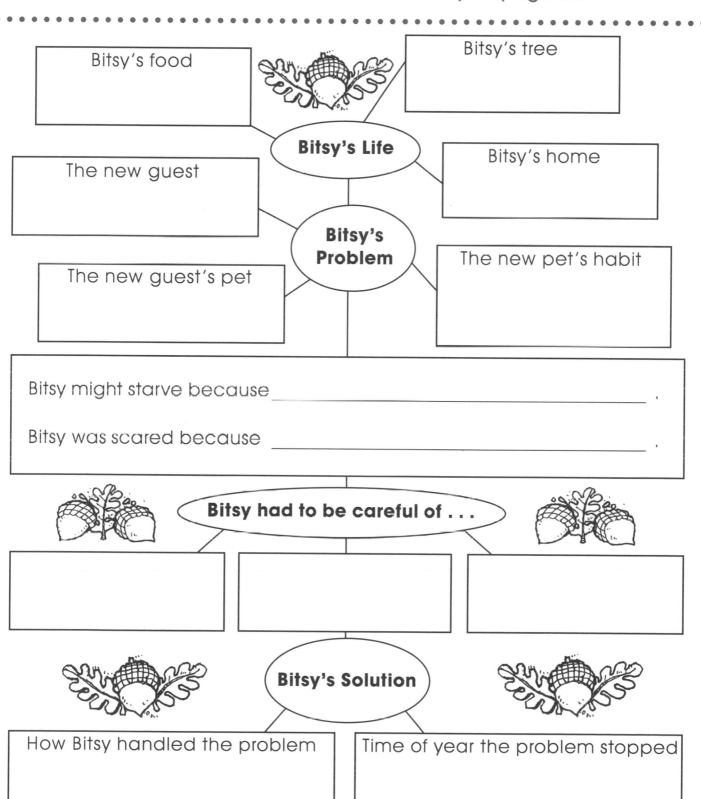

Bitsy's food

Bitsy's tree

Bitsy's Life

The new guest

Bitsy's home

Bitsy's Problem

The new guest's pet

The new pet's habit

Bitsy might starve because _____ .

Bitsy was scared because _____ .

Bitsy had to be careful of . . .

Bitsy's Solution

How Bitsy handled the problem

Time of year the problem stopped

33

The Case of the Missing Heirloom

Read the story. Answer questions about it on page 35.

• •

Dylan waited on the playground in the shade of a big tree. If the other members of the Mystery Society did not arrive soon, he would have to meet the new client alone. Then, he saw Jimmy and Sabena running across the yard. Jimmy reached him first. "Sorry," he gasped. "We just got back from a field trip."

"Okay, well, we should get started," Dylan said. "I got an e-mail this morning from a new boy in the neighborhood. He is in my little brother's class. He has a problem and needs our help."

"Great!" said Sabena. "We haven't had a case all month."

"Actually, we haven't had a case since last year," Jimmy replied.

Sabena shrugged. "So, who's keeping track?"

The group walked to a house in the next block. Dylan pulled out a piece of paper. He checked an address that was written on it. "This is it," he told them. The other two kids followed him up the path to the door.

At the front door, Dylan rang the bell. There was no answer at first. So, he rang the bell again. After a moment, the big door opened. A small boy in a red-striped T-shirt and a pair of jeans stood on the other side. "Are you the Mystery Society?" he asked.

"That's us," Dylan replied. "I'm Dylan, and these are my associates, Jimmy and Sabena. May we come in?"

"Sure," said the boy. "I guess your brother Jack told you about me. I'm Andre, but everybody calls me Dre." He led them to a small TV room and closed the door.

"What is the problem, Dre?" Dylan asked.

"I . . . I lost my grandfather's watch," Dre replied. He looked as though he were about to cry. "If my mom finds out, I don't know what she will do. That watch was worth a lot of money."

"It's okay, Dre," Sabena said gently. "We will help you find it."

"When did you see it last?" Jimmy asked.

"I saw it the day after we moved," Dre said. "It was in the top drawer of my dresser. When I looked for it yesterday, it was gone."

Dre took them upstairs to his room. He pointed to the dresser. Dylan and Jimmy asked Dre more questions. They wanted to know how big the watch was and what it looked like. As Dre described it, Sabena took the top drawer all the way out of the dresser. She reached into the space where the drawer had been. Excitedly, she pulled out the watch. The Mystery Society had cracked another case!

34

Fill in the circle in front of each correct answer.

1. How did Dre hear about the Mystery Society?

   ○ from Dylan's brother

   ○ from Sabena

   ○ from the school newspaper

2. What had Dre lost?

   ○ a pen

   ○ a watch

   ○ 10 dollars

3. How did Dre contact the Mystery Society?

   ○ by e-mail

   ○ by telephone

   ○ through the mail

4. Why were Jimmy and Sabena so late?

   ○ Their teacher made them stay after class.

   ○ They had just come from a field trip.

   ○ They had lost track of time.

5. Why did Dre close the door to the TV room?

   ○ He did not want anyone to leave.

   ○ He wanted to watch TV.

   ○ He did not want his mother to hear.

6. Who solved the mystery?

   ○ Dylan

   ○ Sabena

   ○ Jimmy

Name _____

Two Friends, Two Vacations

Read the two letters. Fill in the chart to contrast the two characters' problems.

• •

Dear Dennis,
    Well, here I am at my aunt's house. How am I ever going to get everything she wants done? I only got to sit down for five minutes before she had me painting the stairs. She wants to wash the walls in the kitchen. She wants me to wax the floor in the hallway. And did I tell you about the barn? She wants me to clean out all the old hay in the barn! It has got to be 100-year-old hay! Every night I fall into bed, and then it feels like I get two minutes of sleep before it is morning again. I sure hope I survive and see you at school in September!

Ralph

Dear Dennis,
    Hey, I miss you! It is so quiet here at my grandmother's house. She does not own a TV! She must be the last person on the planet without one. All morning long, we sit and read, then we eat lunch, then we go for a little walk. After that, we read some more. The only time I get to see anyone is when we shop for groceries. Plus, Grandma will not let me help her with anything. If I offer to wash the dishes, she says, "No, dear, you are on vacation." If I offer to weed the garden, she says, "Oh, no, dear, I always do that." She even makes my bed! I hope I do not die of boredom before school starts!

Sheila

	Ralph	Sheila
1. Where is each friend staying?	_____	_____
2. What is each friend's problem?	_____	_____
3. Describe in one word how each friend feels.	_____	_____
4. How does each friend's letter end?	_____	_____

Name_____

Read the story and answer the questions below. Circle a letter or write the answer for each question.

• •

Report from Fairy Godmother 20010@godmother.com

Subject: Prince Proposes

Cinderella, the subject of Project Number 789-B, is now engaged to the prince. However, I still have a few things to fix before I can leave.

This delay is not my fault. It was caused by Cinderella herself. She simply would not follow orders. Her lateness in leaving the ball caused three serious problems. First of all, I still have not found the mice that were turned into horses. I will try to track them down this week.

Problem number two is solved. We have found the lost glass slipper. But we still have problem number three: we are missing the pumpkin that was made into a coach. I shudder to think what might happen if a pie is made from an enchanted pumpkin. I will report again in one week.

1. Who is the main character in this version of "Cinderella"?_____

2. When does the story take place?

     a. before the ball   b. at the ball   c. after the ball

3. The fairy tale "Cinderella" ends with the prince asking Cinderella to marry him. This story has not ended yet. Why is that?

    a. because Cinderella's slipper is lost

    b. because the ball was not held

    c. because Fairy Godmother 20010 has to fix things that went wrong

4. Name two problems that the fairy godmother still has to solve.

    a. _____

    b. _____

Javier's Bike

Read the story. Answer questions about it on page 39.

• •

Every boy on Javier's block had a bike, and Javier wanted one, too. He often watched his friends ride down to the park. They waved to him as they went by. "Come on, Javier," they called. He just waved back. It was eight long blocks to the park. Walking was very slow, and by the time he got there, it was time to turn around and go back home.

One night, Javier was helping his mother wash dishes. "Please, can I have a bike?" he asked.

His mother shook her head as she handed him a plate to dry. "I'm sorry, Javier. A bike costs a lot of money, and now is not a good time. Your sister needs new shoes, and your grandfather in Mexico is sick. We have to send him money for a doctor. Maybe next year we can buy you a bike."

Javier sighed and finished helping her, then went to his room. He did not want his mother to see how sad he was. He sat down on his bed and stared at the wall. How would he ever get a bike?

Suddenly, he remembered a saying he had heard in class. "Where there is a will, there is a way." It meant that you could get what you wanted. You just had to want it enough to keep trying until you found a way.

The next day was Saturday. Javier was about to walk to the park when he saw Mrs. Martinez next door. She was pulling weeds in her garden. There were too many weeds for her to pull by herself. Her sons had grown up and moved away to other towns, and her husband was away on business. There was no else there who could help her.

Javier said he would help. She smiled and told him to get a pair of gloves, pointing to a shed behind the house. When he opened the door, he saw the gloves. He also saw a bike. It was old and the tires were flat, but it looked beautiful to Javier.

He heard a voice behind him. "That was my youngest son's bike," Mrs. Martinez said. "Do you like it?"

"Oh yes!" replied Javier. He wished that it could be his bike.

"Get the gloves and help me and when we finish, I will give you a cool drink," she said.

Javier picked up the gloves slowly. He turned around to find Mrs. Martinez smiling at him. "And I'll give you the bike too, of course. After all, we can't have you walking to the park every day."

How could he have dreamed that she would give him such a fine gift for such a little favor? Javier grinned from ear to ear. At last, he would have a bike of his own!

Javier's Bike (cont.)

Write answers to the questions on the lines.

• •

1. What did Javier want?

   _____

   _____

   _____

2. Why was he unable to get what he wanted?

   _____

   _____

   _____

3. One Saturday, Javier offered to help someone. Who did he help and why?

   _____

   _____

   _____

4. How did Javier get what he wanted?

   _____

   _____

   _____

A Day on the Trail

Read the two versions of the story below. Then answer the questions on the next page.

● ●

Dylan's story:

Today was the day I had been waiting for—our class nature hike! I was so excited, I got up at five o'clock in the morning. I was the first person on the bus. On the way to the trail, Mr. Evans told us about the different animals, rocks, and plants that we would be looking for, and he gave us each a list to fill out. The person who found the most items on the list would get a prize. It was an excellent, hand-held microscope for fieldwork! Of course, I was determined to win.

A lot of the kids did not understand that they needed to be quiet to see any wildlife. I stayed behind the group and moved very slowly down the trail. A snake slithered right in front of me, and a little red squirrel nearly ran across my foot! I saw a baby rabbit that was eating a leaf bigger than he was. I also saw a robin, two mourning doves, and a blue jay. I found sixteen different leaf specimens and did scratch tests on five different rocks.

I was sorry when we had to leave, but I was thrilled to win the field microscope!

Danny's story:

Today was the day I had been dreading—our class nature hike. My mother could barely drag me out of bed. I hate being outdoors; it is so much more interesting playing computer games. Plus, I always get poison ivy, even if I am miles from the plants!

On the bus, Mr. Evans handed out lists we were supposed to fill in . . . as if the hike itself was not bad enough! I lost my canteen right away; it rolled down a cliff and bounced into the river. Then I ripped my T-shirt on a bush with huge, monster-sized thorns. I did manage to find a couple of rocks, but only because I tripped on them. I am sure there was not a single animal anywhere on the trail. I did not see one. Of course, I did fall down a lot, so maybe I scared them off.

By the time we got back to the bus, I was hot, dirty, and tired. I was so glad to get back to civilization, I nearly hugged my computer. But by bedtime, it was clear that somehow, I had gotten poison ivy again. I was covered with it!

Name _____

Answer the questions about the stories you just read.

• •

Write the name of the character described by each phrase:

1. Thrilled to win the microscope _____

2. Disgusted to find he had poison ivy _____

3. Filled in the whole list _____

4. Found five rocks _____

5. Fell down _____

6. Got up early _____

7. Got up late _____

8. Saw no animals or birds _____

9. Saw a reptile, two animals, and four birds _____

10. Ended the trip tired and dirty _____

11. Ended the trip excited and happy _____

12. Circle the words that describe Dylan's day.

exciting	boring	interesting	good
difficult	happy	bad	tiring

13. Circle the words that describe Danny's day.

scary	itchy	enjoyable	good
difficult	happy	bad	tiring

14. The setting in this story was the same for both, but the two characters re-acted very differently to it. Which character's reaction was most like yours would be? _____ Why? _____

_____

_____

Where Is It?

Read each paragraph below. Choose the correct setting for each story from the Word Bank and write it on the line.

• •

Word Bank
India   USA   The Arctic Circle   Japan   Colonial America

1. Raji felt the sun pounding down on his turban-wrapped head as he tried to make the little elephant obey his commands. But the young one was not learning fast enough. And the festival was only a few days away!
    Raji lives in _____.

2. Keiko smoothed down her kimono. She wanted to look her best. Her family was traveling on a bullet train into the capital city. Keiko could not wait to visit the Tokyo National Museum and walk to the Imperial Palace. She also hoped to see a baseball game and go to a sushi house for dinner. It was going to be a great trip!
    Keiko lives in _____.

3. Manu raised her huge, white head and squinted into the sunlight. Sun meant trouble. Sun meant that the ice she had to cross would be breaking into pieces soon. The polar bear put one paw onto the ice. It felt soft under her foot.
    Manu lives in _____.

4. Ann bent her head over her sewing. She had accidentally poked her finger with the needle. The thread knotted up again. The candle was about to go out. She felt like screaming. But young ladies of the 1700s did not scream. Young ladies sewed well.
    Ann lives in _____.

5. Ian turned on his computer and began to search the Internet for ideas. This year, he wanted to give the best pool party ever. He wanted to provide games with prizes for his guests. He also wanted to serve pizza from the best pizza place in town. When he saw the Web site called "Perfect Pool Parties," he knew he had found the right place to get great ideas.
    Ian lives in _____.

Time and Place

Read the paragraphs. List the setting and problem for each.

• •

Abigail hurried down the path. Sunlight fell through the red and yellow leaves. There was still frost on the fields. Abigail broke into a run because she was late for school. Mrs. McCann had probably already given the spelling test, and there was no way she could make it up.

1. place _____
2. time of day _____
3. time of year _____
4. problem _____

Karen set her backpack on the rock. She wiped her face. It was very hot, and the glare of the sun was hurting her eyes. Everyone had told her not to hike in the desert at this time of year. Karen looked at the sun, which was starting to set. Then she froze. She thought she heard a rattling noise nearby.

5. place _____
6. time of day _____
7. time of year _____
8. problem _____

Joseph's nose was bright red as he stomped into the house. He put his boots on the mat and set his mittens to dry. Then he saw that his backpack was open. His glasses were missing! It was too late to go look for them; it was already dark. He knew that Mom could not afford new ones. What to do?

9. place _____
10. time of day _____
11. time of year _____
12. problem _____
13. Which character do you think has the worst problem? _____
    Why? _____

    _____
    _____
    _____

Name _____

Match Up

Read about the characters. Use the Setting Bank and Problem Bank to find the best setting and problem for each character.

• •

Setting Bank
The home of Mrs. Chu, a cat lover
A park near Betty's home
A street of new houses
A fire station

Problem Bank
A valuable doll is lost in the park.
An owl almost flies into a window.
Mrs. Chu wants to help a stray cat.
A dog wants his old job back.

Emily Ann wears a long blue dress, a blue bonnet, and a knitted shawl. Her head is made of china, and her shoes are real leather. Emily Ann has lived with the same family for almost two hundred years. But her new owner, Betty, is careless and forgetful.

1. Problem: _____
2. Setting: _____

Zak is white with black spots. He wears a red leather collar. Zak used to have a job. He was trained to run to the truck whenever the alarm bell went off. He has just started a new life as a pet in the fire chief's family, but he is not happy.

3. Problem: _____
4. Setting: _____

James does not have a home. His orange fur is matted, and his white paws are gray with mud. James is scared of people. He has found a house where a bowl of tuna fish sits on the step every morning. Sometimes he thinks that someone watches him while he eats.

5. Problem: _____
6. Setting: _____

Shera lives in a place that used to have lots of trees. Now, people are building there. Shera is finding it harder and harder to find food. One night, she goes out hunting and almost flies into a big glass window. She turns away just in time. In the future, she will have to be more careful.

7. Problem: _____
8. Setting: _____

What Is the Story?

Circle the answers to the questions about story elements.

· ·

Juan is reading a book about dogs. It is called *Ezra, Wonder Dog of Mapleville.* In Mapleville, a group of dogs leads people to safety after the dam breaks and their town is flooded. At the end of the story, the mayor of Mapleville gives one dog a medal for saving his pet cat from the floodwaters.

1. Who do you think is the main character in Juan's book?

    a. Mr. Lee, the mayor of Mapleville

    b. Tyler, the child who is rescued

    c. Ezra, a Great Dane

2. What do you think the climax of the story might be?

    a. Ezra and other dogs wake their owners when they hear the dam starting to break in the night.

    b. Mayor Lee awards the Helping Hand medal to a brave dog.

    c. After the townspeople have climbed the hills to safety, the mayor's pet falls into the floodwaters.

    d. The townspeople struggle to find safe paths into the hills, and are helped by a group of brave dogs.

    e. Ezra is given a lifetime supply of dog food from the Mapleville Supermarket.

3. What do you think the problem might be in Juan's book?

    a. Mapleville has too many dogs.

    b. Mapleville is near a dam that is not strong enough.

    c. Mapleville gets too much rain.

    d. Mapleville is surrounded by dangerous hills.

4. Which would **not** be an event in Juan's book?

    a. Mapleville schoolchildren put on a play about brave dogs for the town.

    b. Ezra gets to go to obedience school and learn lots of new commands.

    c. The people of Mapleville decide to make a law to get rid of all the dogs in their town.

    d. The whole town has a parade for Ezra, the Wonder Dog.

45

Answer Key

Page 4
1. Brenda; 2. Betty; 3. Billy; 4. Brad;
5. Billy; 6. Brenda; 7. Brad; 8. Betty

Page 5
a. 2; b. 6; c. 1; d. 5; e. 4; f. 3

Page 7
1. Ahmad; 2. Valerie; 3. Timothy;
4. Sara; 5. a. Timothy, b. Sara,
c. Ahmad, d. Valerie; 6. Answers will
vary.

Page 8
Circle: 1. Goldilocks; 2. Officer Grizzly
and Officer Paws; 3. Officer Grizzly;
4. Baby Bear; 5. Papa Bear; 6. Officer
Paws

Page 9
Answers will vary, but the words
spider, jar, apartment, rain, and
afternoon should appear at least
once.

Page 11
Sample responses: 1. She is very sad
to leave. 2. No; she does not talk
to the other children in the wagon
train. 3. She began to feel better.
4. scared, shy, obedient, homesick;
5. wide, fast, dangerous; 6. to buy
cheaper land; 7. Answers will vary.
8. Answers will vary.

Page 12
1. from winter to spring; 2. the North
Pole; 3. It is very cold and snowy.
4. He builds a bear out of snow, puts
a scarf and hat on it, and places a
blanket and toys beside it.

Page 13
1. winter; 2. Egyptian desert;
3. summer; 4. autumn; 5. medieval
England; 6. ancient Rome

Page 15
1. New World; 2. There are no
buildings or shops. 3. He knows every
tree in the forest. 4. He has heard
stories about her people, and she
does not know about his tribe.
5. Wehanta would not be a
character in the story.

Page 16
1. a wolf; 2. buying clothes; 3. A boy
climbs a giant beanstalk to a castle
in the sky. 4. Settings Can Create
Adventures.

Page 17
Underline: 1. Then he glanced at his
wristwatch; 2. He looked up as he
heard the weather report on the
radio. 3. "I have news for you, my
lord," he said, holding out a text
message. 4. She drew the oil lamp
closer and started typing. 5. The
servants hurried to set up strings of
tiny electric lights across the mantle.
6. b; 7. c; 8. a; 9. d